LIFE AND TIMES IN
ANCIENT
ROME

KINGFISHER

KINGFISHER

Kingfisher Publications Plc
New Penderel House
283–288 High Holborn
London WC1V 7HZ
www.kingfisherpub.com

Based on material first published in the Sightseers series
by Kingfisher Publications Plc 2000

This edition first published by Kingfisher Publications Plc 2007
2 4 6 8 10 9 7 5 3 1

1TR/0607/TIMS/(MA)/14OMA/C

Written and edited by: Conrad Mason, Jonathan Stroud
Consultant: David Nightingale
Production controller: Aysun Ackay
DTP manager: Nicky Studdart

Illustrations by: Inklink Firenze and Kevin Maddison

A CIP catalogue record for this book
is available from the British Library.

ISBN 978 0 7534 1558 0 (paperback)
ISBN 978 0 7534 1627 3 (hardback)

Printed in China

Contents

The city of Rome

At the time of its foundation, Rome was little more than a few farmers' houses on an Italian hillside, but it grew to become the head of the largest empire the world had ever seen. Rome ruled over people from places as far apart as Britain and Egypt, but the city remained the heart of the empire, home to a million people at the height of its power. But while riches poured into the city, nearly a quarter of the population was out of work and relied on free grain.

◁ By 128CE the empire was so big that the emperor Hadrian (76–138CE) spent most of his time away from Rome, protecting the empire's boundaries. This book is about the city of Rome in Hadrian's time.

According to legend, Rome was founded in 753BCE by Romulus and Remus. It was said that they were brought up by a wolf.

For centuries, Rome was ruled by a Senate of the most important men. The eagle became the symbol of Rome.

Rome's first rival was the African city of Carthage. In 218BCE it invaded Rome with elephants, but was defeated.

▽ In the Forum stood the Rostra, a platform from which important political speeches were made.

Rostra

Senate House

The city's spiritual heart was the Forum, or market place. When Rome was just a village, its people met in this open space to trade and discuss politics. By the time of Hadrian the old square had been built up with giant temples and political memorials, and the markets moved elsewhere. The Senate House stood by the Forum, but the real centre of power was the emperor's palace nearby.

◁ Rome was a city of extremes. It was full of spacious palaces and public buildings, but was extremely crowded, with very narrow streets. A tiny elite was staggeringly rich, but a third of Rome's inhabitants were slaves.

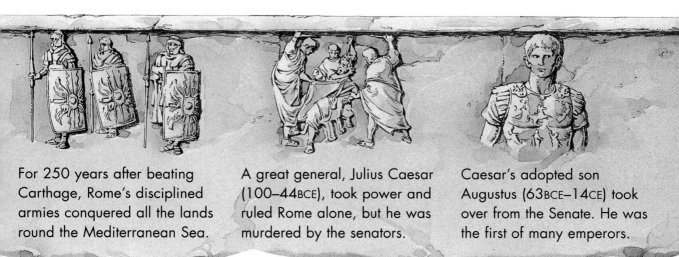

For 250 years after beating Carthage, Rome's disciplined armies conquered all the lands round the Mediterranean Sea.

A great general, Julius Caesar (100–44BCE), took power and ruled Rome alone, but he was murdered by the senators.

Caesar's adopted son Augustus (63BCE–14CE) took over from the Senate. He was the first of many emperors.

Roman transport

The Romans needed excellent transport and communication to keep control over their empire, so they constructed a vast network of long, straight highways. This road system was built by the Roman army, and stretched over more than 50,000 kilometres in total. It was possible to travel from one end to the other in 100 days on horseback. Inside Rome itself it was easy to get lost – none of the thousands of winding streets had names or numbers.

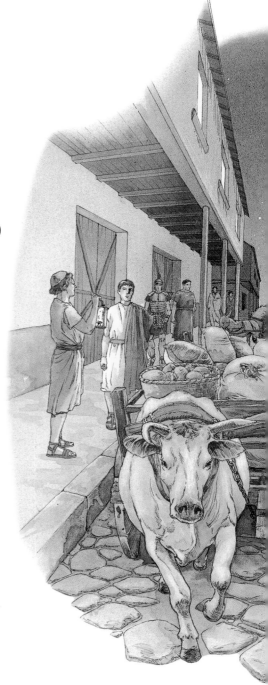

△ The River Tiber in Rome was a major transport route, with merchant ships sailing to and from the coast, bringing grain, wine and other supplies.

▷ Romans built roads with hard-wearing foundations. A flat layer of sand went on the bottom, with layers of stone and gravel above. The road was topped with paving stones, which were curved to let rain run off. Engineers had tools to keep the road straight so that journeys would take as little time as possible.

▽ With no street names, citizens
found their way around Rome by
using temples and statues as landmarks.

◁ Wealthy
Romans had
teams of slaves
to carry them
around the city.

In Rome the roads were covered
with mud, rubbish and sewage.
Raised pavements and stepping
stones helped people keep their feet
dry, and the wealthy travelled by
sedan chair. Streets were busy even
at night, as traders with noisy,
slow-moving carts were only allowed
into the city at dusk. Citizens who
went out at night would often take
a slave with them for protection –
muggers and thieves were common.

Clothing

To a Roman it was very important to have the latest hairstyle and clothing. Fashions changed often. For instance, Roman men were clean-shaven until the emperor Hadrian started a trend for wearing beards. Men usually wore tunics, but had robes called togas for important occasions.

△ Rich women had personal slaves to shape their hair into elaborate styles. This could take all morning. Others wore wigs made from the hair of foreign slaves. Blonde hair from German women was thought to be very exotic.

◁ Romans used various tools to help improve their looks. These included combs, hairpins, tweezers for plucking hairs, and even small spoons for scooping wax out of ears.

▽ Both men and women wore jewellery, including brooches to hold up their cloaks. The rich had rings, bracelets and necklaces made out of gold or silver, while the poor had bronze jewellery. The finest pieces were set with precious stones from the furthest parts of the empire.

◁ For women, a pale face was a sign of status. Poor women had rough, red faces from working outside. Many Romans used creams made of chalk, flour and lead to whiten their skin.

Wealthy men showed their status by wearing long tunics. Poor men and slaves had short tunics which were more practical and gave their legs more freedom as they worked. A fashionable Roman woman took great care with her clothes. She would wear an ankle-length woollen under-tunic, with a colourful embroidered dress, or *stola*, on top. This was made out of wool, cotton or silk.

Food and drink

Rich Romans enjoyed an unending array of exotic delicacies – from stuffed dormice to ostrich and flamingo. The poor made do with grain boiled into porridge and mixed with cheap foods like eggs and cheese. For these Romans, meat was a rare dish. Wine mixed with water was the usual drink for all citizens, rich and poor alike. It was considered vulgar to drink undiluted wine. *Cena*, or dinner, was the biggest meal of the day.

△ For most Romans, breakfast and lunch were light meals that could be eaten quickly while standing up.

△ Roman cooks used strong, spicy sauces and herbs to cover the rotting taste of old meat or fish. The Romans' favourite sauce was *liquamen*, which was strained from salted fish guts left out in the sun.

In Rome many people did not cook at all, since ovens were banned in the crowded tenement buildings because of the risk of fire. Instead, people visited stalls and taverns to buy soup, sausages, pies, fried fish and fruit.

▽ Many hosts saw a party as a great opportunity to show off their wealth and impress the guests with fine silverware.

The richest Romans held splendid dinner parties. Guests reclined on three couches around a table, supporting themselves with their left elbow, and holding their food in their right hand. They rarely used knives or spoons, so the food served was easy to pick up and not too hot. The host's slaves served everyone, but guests sometimes brought their own slaves along to help out.

▷ Guests at big banquets ate huge quantities of food. Salads and oysters were brought out for starters, followed by several courses of game birds, boar, venison, hare, ham and fish. Meals ended with honey cakes and fruit. Sometimes guests made themselves sick so they could fit more food into their stomachs.

Shopping in Rome

Every day ships and wagons arrived in Rome from all over the empire, carrying goods made in distant corners of the world. Traders from as far as India and China brought luxury silks and spices to delight the wealthy buyers. The city's bustling markets and shops offered almost anything for sale, from basics such as grain, pots and clothing to beautiful vases, skilled slaves and elegant jewellery.

▷ Rome was the richest city in the empire, and luxury goods were plentiful. This vase, made out of blue and white glass, would have taken months to make, and could only be afforded by the very rich.

Most Roman shops were stalls or rooms opening out on to the street. The owners usually lived in the room above and drew wooden shutters across the front to keep out thieves during the night. There was a wide variety of exotic things on sale: wool from Britain, silver from Spain, carpets from Turkey and perfumes from Iran. The same coinage was used across the whole empire, from Asia Minor to Britain, but goods were at their most expensive in Rome itself.

◁ Trajan's Market near the Forum was a massive semi-circular shopping centre carved out of the side of a hill, with 150 shops, offices and a central open space where traders set up stalls.

▽ Most citizens only went shopping for expensive one-off items. Shopping for food and other essentials was done by male slaves.

▽ Slaves were brought in from conquered lands. Those who could cook, dance or sing were worth far more than those without any skills.

By far the most important thing on sale was grain – imported daily from Africa, since Italian farmers could not produce enough wheat to feed Rome by themselves. In hard times, the emperor gave free hand-outs of grain to the needy.

13

Homes

The city of Rome sprawled over seven hills. The richest people lived in spacious villas on the airy higher ground, while everyone else was crammed into ramshackle blocks of flats in the valleys below. In the summer these hot and over-crowded streets were a breeding-ground for disease, and the few who could afford it left the city to stay in the countryside.

▽ Buildings were arranged in blocks called *insulae*, meaning 'islands', divided up by the grid of roads. In many places the streets were so narrow that it was possible to shake hands with someone in the opposite building.

◁ A fire in an *insula* spread quickly and was very dangerous. Rome had seven squads of professional firemen, the *vigiles*, whose job was to fight fires. They also helped keep order in the rowdy streets.

Most of Rome's people lived in small rented rooms in large, crowded tenement buildings. These stuffy flats were vulnerable to fire and were so poorly made that they often fell down. Each block had up to six storeys, and had shops on the ground floor. The noise of traders' carts kept people awake for much of the night, except for those who lived at the very top of the building.

A rich man's house was built around the *atrium*, an open hall with a hole in the ceiling and a pool in the centre to catch rainwater. Doors to the dining room, reception rooms, kitchen and bedrooms led off on each side. The *atrium* was the house's main source of light and air – outside walls had few windows, to keep out noise and burglars. At the back of the house was a *peristyle*, a garden filled with shrubs and statues.

△ Even big houses had little furniture. The couches in the dining room were the most important items. Adding a woollen blanket meant they doubled up as beds at night.

▷ Many houses had small shrines where families worshipped their own personal gods, called *lares*. Every day they left offerings of wine, cakes and incense at the shrines, which contained tiny statues of the *lar*. Offerings were meant to bring wealth and happiness to the household.

The baths

The public baths were an essential part of life in Rome. People visited the baths to relax, swim, chat and play games in magnificent surroundings. There were hundreds of baths in the city, and many people visited one every day. Most trips were free, because rich men paid everyone's fees in the hope of gaining votes or increasing their popularity.

△ Romans cleaned themselves at the baths by rubbing oil into their skin, and then scraping off the mingled oil and dirt with a blunt metal tool called a *strigil*.

▷ Water for the baths was heated by underground furnaces. This meant that the tiles on the floor could be scalding hot. Visitors wore sandals to protect their feet.

▽ Men and women bathed at separate times. A bell was rung to signal the changeover.

▽ The floors of baths were covered in intricate mosaics. This one from Pompeii shows an octopus surrounded by fish.

▽ All the baths were very richly decorated. The rooms were lined with marble pillars, and the ceilings were high and beautifully painted. This luxury gave even poor people a regular taste of the power and wealth of Rome.

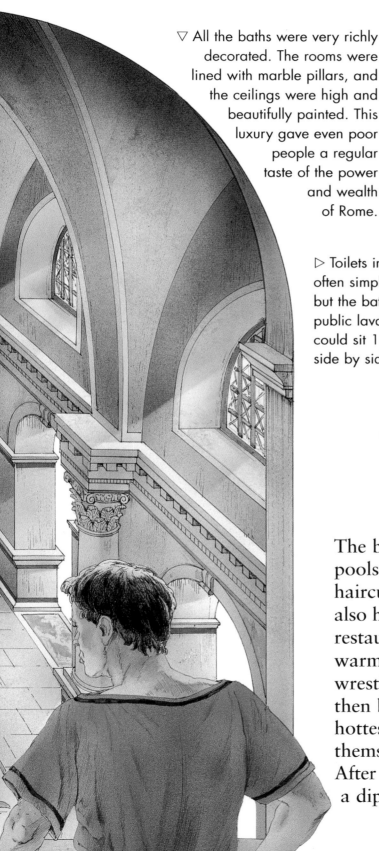

▷ Toilets in Roman homes were often simply pots in the corner, but the baths had splendid public lavatories. Some could sit 16 people side by side.

The baths included hot and cold pools, steam rooms, saunas and haircutting salons. The largest ones also had forecourts with shops, restaurants and libraries. Visitors warmed up in the gymnasium by wrestling or playing ball games, and then bathed in the *caldarium* – the hottest room of all – to bring themselves out in a cleansing sweat. After a massage, they finished with a dip in the ice-cold plunge pool.

The theatre

Visiting the theatre was a favourite pastime. Semi-circular stone theatres hosted plays and games, often to celebrate recent military victories. The Romans got their love of drama from the Greeks, but although some Greek tragedies were shown, most Romans preferred comedy. The action was fast, with lots of crude jokes and happy endings. Some characters were very popular, such as the cunning slave who always managed to talk himself out of trouble in the nick of time.

▽ Roman audiences were very noisy. If they were pleased, they clapped their hands, snapped their fingers and thumbs and waved their togas. If not, they hissed, shouted and made rude noises.

△ Actors rehearsed in the building behind the stage. They were all men, but they played women's roles too.

Romans loved special effects and big spectacles. Ghosts appeared through holes in the stage floor and winches helped to produce gods from above. In some tragedies, a real-life criminal was brought on stage and executed. There was little scenery, although real chariots and horses sometimes appeared on stage. Actors wore masks, wigs and special colours that showed what kind of character they were playing.

▽ Roman comedies usually had lots of movement to keep the audience's attention, with characters chasing each other, falling over or performing acrobatics.

▷ Music and songs accompanied the plays. Greek instruments such as the stringed lyre or *cithara* were popular, as well as the double pipes, cymbals and tambourine.

Circus Maximus

Chariot-racing was the most popular sport in Rome, and in the time of Hadrian, the Circus Maximus was the biggest stadium in the world. Up to 250,000 people could crowd in to see the races – more than half of the city's population! Citizens supported one of the four teams, the Blues, Whites, Reds or Greens. Entry was free to watch all 24 races in a day.

△ Betting on chariot races and gladiator fights was allowed, but all other gambling was illegal. Many Romans went to secret betting houses, where they could wager money on dice or on the toss of a coin.

△ Cheating was common. Drivers sometimes slipped a stick through their rivals' spokes to make them crash.

The race began when an official dropped a handkerchief. There were seven 1.5km laps of the wall, or *spina*, at the centre of the arena. On top of the *spina* were seven metal dolphins – one was removed to mark each lap.

△ Chariot races were popular with both rich and poor Romans. Children from wealthy families had small chariots to play in, pulled by donkeys or goats.

Chariots were light and mobile, but were also flimsy and could easily overturn. The most dangerous parts of the course were the corners, where drivers had to turn at high speeds. Collisions were common, as drivers tried to force opponents into the wall. Each driver tied the reins around his waist so that he had his hands free to whip the horses. This meant that if he crashed, he could easily be dragged to his death.

The Colosseum

On public holidays, citizens enjoyed watching savage blood sports in the Colosseum. This was the biggest amphitheatre in the empire, and played host to spectacular and extremely violent entertainment. There was everything from mock sea battles to public executions, with slaves and criminals being eaten alive by wild beasts.

△ Exotic animals were imported from all over the world. They were usually killed in huge mock hunting displays. However, ferocious lions were often used to devour helpless criminals.

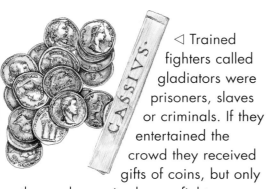

◁ Trained fighters called gladiators were prisoners, slaves or criminals. If they entertained the crowd they received gifts of coins, but only those who survived many fights were set free. These lucky few were given bone tablets with their names on to prove that they were free men.

The Colosseum had 80 entrances so that people could find seats quickly. There was also a canvas awning which could be pulled over the top to protect spectators from the sun. This was operated by teams of slaves who pulled on ropes outside. Underneath were underground chambers where gladiators and animals were kept.

Gladiator fights were the most popular entertainment in the Colosseum. There were several different types of fighter, each with their own weapons and armour. Most fights were to the death, but a beaten gladiator could appeal to the emperor to save his life. If he had fought bravely, the emperor gave a thumbs up to let him live. If not, a thumbs down was the signal for his opponent to kill him.

▽ The nimble *retiarius* had a net to snare his enemy, and a trident to stab him. The *secutor* was heavily armoured, making him powerful but slow.

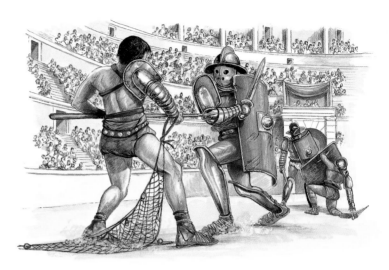

▽ Heavy helmets offered protection, but they were difficult to see out of. This was a serious disadvantage against fast opponents.

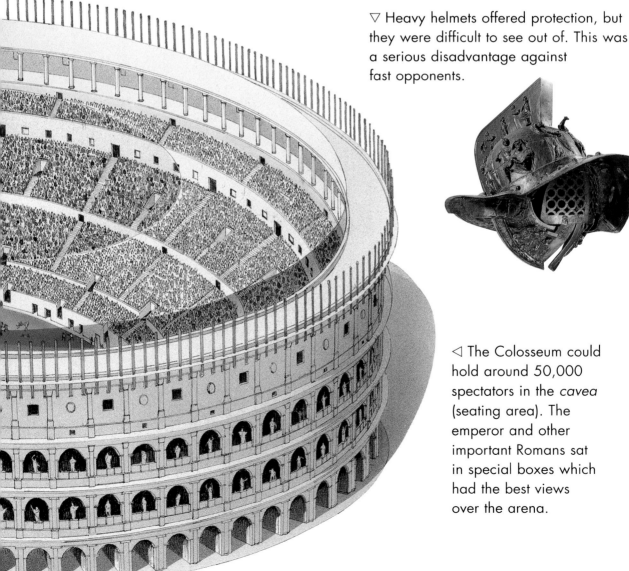

◁ The Colosseum could hold around 50,000 spectators in the *cavea* (seating area). The emperor and other important Romans sat in special boxes which had the best views over the arena.

Temples and worship

Romans believed in many different gods. They thought that everything from personal health to success in war depended on the gods' favour, and that regular rituals had to be carried out to keep them satisfied. In hundreds of temples across the city, priests elected from among the nobles performed sacrifices on behalf of the people. Festivals and feast days were held for each god, and offerings of fruit, wine and animals were made every day.

▽ Jupiter was the king of the gods, and Rome itself was thought to be under his protection. The Romans had gods to watch over every aspect of their lives. Some of the most important were Mars, god of war, Apollo, the god of light and music, Vesta, the goddess of home and hearth, and Minerva, the goddess of wisdom.

▷ Hadrian built a great temple to all the gods – the Pantheon. It was a masterpiece of engineering, with a vast dome and statues of the gods lining the walls. A single hole at the top, the *oculus*, provided light and represented the sun.

▽ Priests often sacrificed animals to the gods. The more willingly they went to the slaughter, the better the omen. Once dead, the entrails were studied. If they were in good condition, the body was cooked and eaten.

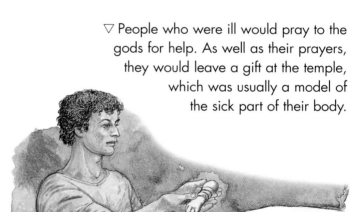

▽ People who were ill would pray to the gods for help. As well as their prayers, they would leave a gift at the temple, which was usually a model of the sick part of their body.

Romans looked to the gods whenever they had an important decision to make. Thunder, lightning and the behaviour of birds were studied by special priests called augurs, who looked for omens – signs from the gods – which would tell them what was going to happen in the future.

The countryside

Although Rome was the capital of the empire, the Italian countryside surrounding it was also important. For the rich it provided a refuge from the bustle of the city. Vast farming estates of wealthy families supplied much of the food that kept Rome going, as well as plenty of wine and olive oil. These products were carried in huge quantities to ports on the Mediterranean coast and exported by sea all over the empire.

▽ Merchant sailing vessels were heavy and slow. They had a square sail and two great steering oars at the stern. Oil and wine were carried in large pottery jars called *amphorae*.

◁ Just 25km from the city at the mouth of the River Tiber was Rome's great port of Ostia. Massive warehouses on the seafront stored grain, wine and olive oil before barges brought them up the river and into Rome.

▽ Most rich families only visited the estates in the summer to get out of the sweltering city. But there was a workforce of slaves on the farms all year round who tended to the crops and livestock.

At the heart of a farming estate was the nobleman's villa, surrounded by vineyards and houses for slaves and workers. In the autumn, slaves picked the grapes and crushed them to extract the juice. This was poured into large, half-buried jars to ferment and become wine. The jars were sealed with pitch to keep out rain. Poor-quality grapes were made into wine for the workers.

△ When the olives had been harvested from the trees, they were piled into an olive press. Slaves pulled the handles down to squash the olives and squeeze the oil out into a jar.

The countryside was crisscrossed with gigantic aqueducts running to Rome from distant water sources. They supplied over 180 million litres of water to the city every day, mostly to baths and fountains. The water moved by gravity, so each aqueduct was angled downhill along its entire length. Stone slabs covered the water channel to keep out any dirt.

Living in Rome

Life in Rome was hard for all but the very rich. Laws were enforced with tough punishments, and citizens were expected to obey a rigid social hierarchy. Those who fell ill or were injured went to see doctors who had little scientific knowledge. Often there was not enough food for the poor.

◁ Magistrates were one of the few officials elected by Rome's citizens. These rich men spent massive sums of money on pleasing the people and winning their support.

Medicine was based largely on herbal remedies and was not always effective. For broken ribs, for example, the writer Pliny recommended applying a mix of goat's dung and wine to the wound.

Roman society followed a very strict hierarchy. At the top were Roman citizens, who were divided into the wealthy nobility and the ordinary people, or *plebeians*. Non-citizens from outside Rome had fewer rights. Below all these were the slaves, who did most of the work in farms and in the city, and had almost no rights at all.

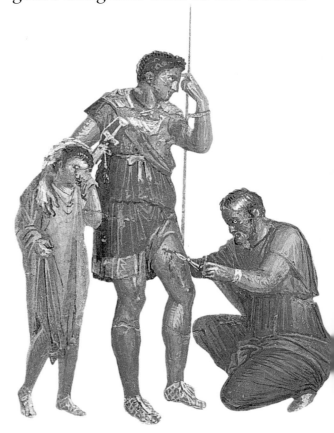

△ Surgeons had sophisticated tools to operate on wounds and broken bones, but the only painkillers were poppy juice and wine.

▽ Four squads of special legionaries were assigned to carry out police duties in Rome. In times of serious disturbance, the Praetorian Guard were called in.

The Romans were keen on discipline and dealt with criminals severely. Minor crimes were punished by beatings. Thieves were branded. For the worst offences, slaves could be executed by crucifixion. An elite force of legionaries, the Praetorian Guard, had the job of protecting the emperor. No other legions were allowed near Rome, so that the emperor could not be overthrown.

The emperor appointed the most important officials, who were all nobles. Rich young men became lawyers and magistrates, before being appointed as governors of far-flung regions of the empire.

◁ Some slaves were made to wear special tags with their master's name and address on. If they ran away, they could be caught and returned.

Quiz

At its height, Rome was the most vibrant and exciting city in the ancient world. Try this quiz to find out how much you can remember about life in Rome. Answers can be found on page 32.

1. The Forum was one of the oldest parts of Rome. How did it first start out?

a) As a hilltop fortress.

b) As a market place in a village.

c) As a temple to Romulus, founder of Rome.

2. What creature cared for Romulus as a baby?

a) A wolf.

b) A bear.

c) An eagle.

3. What was most likely to keep people awake at night in the streets of Rome?

a) Traders' carts bringing goods into the city.

b) All-night chariot races through the streets.

c) Drunken revellers.

4. What did Roman women make wigs out of?

a) Horse hair from Arabian stallions.

b) Human hair from slaves.

c) Finely spun silk from the Far East.

5. Why would a Roman woman want to have a pale face?

a) It proved she was of pure Roman blood.

b) It was thought to be a sign of good health.

c) It proved that she was rich enough to stay indoors and not do any work.

6. Goods came to Rome from all over the empire. What was the most vital import?

a) Swords brought from Asia Minor.

b) Grain imported from Africa.

c) Tea cups from Britain.

30

7. What was *liquamen*?

a) A mix of rotting fish guts and salt that the Romans used as a sauce.

b) A strong alcoholic drink that was made from cranberries.

c) A mix of boars' droppings and wine used to treat bad chest injuries.

8. A *retiarius* was one of the most popular types of gladiator. What kind of weapons did he carry?

a) A net and a trident.

b) A short sword and a heavy rectangular shield.

c) A light javelin and a round shield.

9. The *lares* were very important to most Romans. Who were they?

a) Rome's special fire brigade.

b) The chief priests of Jupiter who worked at the Pantheon.

c) Household gods who watched over the family.

10. How did charioteers know how many laps were left in the Circus Maximus?

a) A track marshal waved a flag with a number written on it.

b) They had to remember themselves.

c) The laps were counted with metal dolphins.

11. Romans loved going to the theatre. What kind of play did they most like to see?

a) Greek tragedies, with plenty of death and sorrow.

b) Fast-paced comedies, with lots of farcical situations and silly jokes.

c) Political satires, filled with angry jokes at the emperor's expense.

Index

Acknowledgements

Inklink Firenze illustrators
Simone Boni, Alessandro Rabatti, Lorenzo Pieri, Luigi Critone, Lucia Mattioli, Francisco Petracchi, Theo Caneschi, Federico Ferniani, Alain Bressan, Concetta D'Amato.

Additional illustrations
Richard Berridge, Luigi Galante, Nicki Palin, Thomas Troyer.

Picture credits
b = bottom, c = centre, l = left, r = right, t = top
p.4cl The Bridgeman Art Library, London/New York/Museo Archeologico Nazionale, Naples; p.6cl AKG London/Erich Lessing; p.9tr The British Museum; c Scala; p.11tr The Bridgeman Art Library, London/New York/Louvre, Paris, France; p.12c Ancient Art & Architecture; p.15br The British Museum; p.17tr Ancient Art & Architecture; p.19tl Ancient Art & Architecture; p.20bl C M Dixon/British Museum; p.23tl Giraudon/Louvre, Paris; p.25cr AKG London/Museum für Deutsche Geschichte, Berlin; p.27cr AKG London/Erich Lessing; p.28br Scala

The publisher would like to thank the following for permission to reproduce their material. Every care has been taken to trace copyright holders. However, if there have been unintentional omissions or failure to trace copyright holders, we apologize and will, if informed, endeavour to make corrections in any future edition.

Quiz answers

1 b) 2 a) 3 a) 4 b) 5 c) 6 b) 7 a) 8 a) 9 c) 10 c) 11 b)